ALCOHOLICS ANONYMOUS BIG BOOK WORKBOOK

(Revised February 2015)

By George B

Introduction

The book Alcoholics Anonymous is the basic textbook of Alcoholics Anonymous. The first 164 pages have remained the same since the book was first published in 1939. The rest of the book contains personal stories of people who have recovered from alcoholism by following the *"suggestions"* in the book. This workbook is intended to be a guide for studying the text and applying it to the reader's own life.

Every attempt has been made to follow the text and not to deviate from the written words. The workbook is a personal workbook and each person is encouraged to write in the "NOTES" pages following each chapter the things that are gotten from what the chapter contains.

The stories are intended by the original writers of the book to help others see some of themselves in each story and hopefully learn from them.

The author of this workbook is just another recovered alcoholic who is hoping to help other alcoholics in their own recovery. There are prayers said every day for those who use this workbook that they improve their own sobriety by using it.

George B

Table of Contents

17. Personal Stories

4th Edition

How Forty-One Alcoholics

Recovered from their Malady

Part I – Pioneers of AA

Part II – They Stopped in Time

Part III – They Lost Nearly All

1. Forward – First Edition

1. What is the main purpose of the book *Alcoholics Anonymous*?

2. What is meant by the phrase: *Precisely how we have recovered*?

3. Why did the original authors of the book wish to remain anonymous?

4. Why did they choose not to be an organization on the conventional sense of the word?

5. What was meant by"inquiries by scientific, medical and religious will be welcome?

2. Forward – Second Edition

1. What was the "miracle" that took place since the book was first published in 1939?

2. What growth took place in AA over the sixteen years between the First Edition and the Second Edition of this book?

3. What did Bill W learn from Dr. Silkworth?

4. What realization did Bill W have in Akron?

5. What was discovered in the alcoholic ward of the Akron Hospital?

6. What convinced the early members of AA that a new light had entered the world of the alcoholic?

7. How did AA get to be called *Alcoholics Anonymous*?

8. What was the "test" that faced the society of AA during its fearsome and exciting adolescent period/

9. What principles had to evolve so that AA could survive and function effectively?

10. When were the Twelve Traditions confirmed?

11. What was another main reason for the acceptance of AA that helped it make progress so rapidly during the initial growth of AA?

12. What is the hope of Alcoholics *Anonymous* for those who have not yet found an answer for their alcoholism?

3. Forward – Third Edition

1. What was the worldwide membership and number of groups in how many countries 1n 1976?

2. What was the percentage of women members?

3. How does *Alcoholics Anonymous* increase in size?

4. Forward – Fourth Edition

1. How many people were estimated to be in *Alcoholics Anonymous* in 2001?

2. What has played a major role in AA's growth?

3. Do you think the founding members of AA had any idea of the number and variety of people who would be joining AA? Explain.

4. Face-to-face, modem-to-modem, what language do all alcoholics speak?

5. The Doctor's Opinion

1. What physician wrote a letter endorsing the work of AA?

2. What convinced this physician that the approach of AA works?

3. What did this physician say about the *"remedy"* developed by the early members of AA?

4. What did this doctor's theory say about the body of the alcoholic?

5. Why must a man or woman's brain be cleared before he or she be approached about the spiritual solution for their alcoholism?

6. What did the doctor mean by the term *"moral psychology"*?

7. How does he explain the phenomenon of craving?

8. Have you experienced the condition in which you could not distinguish the true from the false?

9. What kind of *"psychic change"* must occur if there is any hope of recovery?

10. What happens once the psychic change has occurred?

11. What *"power"* is needed to effect this psychic check?

12. What is the *"supreme sacrifice"* some men and women make rather than continue to fight?

13. What are some of the kinds of people who cannot stay sober?

14. Why are some alcoholics doomed?

15. What is the phenomenon which cannot be overcome?

16. Describe the two examples of successful recoveries and what did they have in common?

17. What do you think Dr. Silkworth meant by: *"I earnestly advise every alcoholic to read this book through, and, though perhaps he came to scoff, he may remain to pray?"*

18. What is meant by **"contempt prior to investigation"**?

Chapter One - Bill's Story

1. What was the ominous warning that Bill W encountered when he visited Winchester Cathedral?

2. What happened when Bill W was facing examinations in law school?

3. What occurred with Bill's drinking as he experienced financial success?

4. What did Bill do when the stock market collapsed?

5. What did Bill do when he was broke, after having such financial success on Wall Street?

6. What finally cause Bill to realize that he was powerless over alcohol?

7. What convinced Bill that self-knowledge was not the answer to hi drinking problem?

8. What came over Bill when he was told to choose his own conception of God?

9. What could be built on a foundation of complete willingness?

10. What did Bill offer to God?

11. Are we asked to do the same thing in our own personal program? Explain.

12. What did Bill sense and feel when he fully accepted the spiritual proposals?

13. What have the people in AA found for themselves?

Chapter Two - There is a Solution

1. What Bill discovered about the AA Program is that you cannot keep it unless you give it away. List situations in your sober life where this has actually happened to you.

2. What is the *"tremendous fact"* that all of us in AA discover?

3. What is unique about our alcoholic illness?

4. Who does it affect besides ourselves?

5. None of us make a sole vocation of this work, nor do we think our effectiveness would be improved if we did. What is that *"work"*? Explain.

6. What did the early members of AA decide to do about carrying the message to the alcoholic who is still suffering?

7. If you are an alcoholic who wants to get over it, you may already be asking yourself what I have to do and what is the purpose of this book. What do you have to do and what do you think the purpose of this book is?

8. What kind of people do not understand our problem?

9. What characterizes the *"real alcoholic"*?

10. Why does he or she behave like this?

11. When he (or she) takes any alcohol whatsoever, what happens?

12. Where does the main problem of the alcoholic center?

13. What is the truth about why does he (or she) takes that first drink?

14. At a certain point in his drinking, he passes into what state?

15. What has he (or she) lost?

16. Why is he (or she) without defense against that first drink?

17. What are the stark, ugly facts about alcoholism?

18. What is the solution?

19. What is the *"great fact"* that we have discovered?

20. Explain why there is no middle-of the-road solution for our alcoholism?

21. What is the certain, simple attitude that an alcoholic **must** maintain?

22. What did the doctor tell the man about his religious convictions?

23. What is the *"Design for Living"* that we have been given?

24. What is in the stories at the end of the book that persuades us to say, *"Yes, I must be one of them also. I must have this thing"*?

Chapter Three - More About Alcoholism

1. What have most of us been unwilling to admit?

2. What do we have to concede to our innermost selves and why do we have to admit it?

3. Is there any such thing as making a "normal" drinker out of an alcoholic?

4. What methods have you used to try to prove to yourself that you were not an alcoholic?

5. Who diagnoses that a person is an alcoholic and why is it that person?

6. Does your story sound at all like the man who is talked about in the book dodging streetcars, and if not, what is yours like?

7. Have you seen the truth that *"once an alcoholic, always an alcoholic"*? Describe yourself.

8. How do we stop drinking completely?

9. What are some of the mental states that precede the *first* drink?

10. What is the precise definition of the word *insanity* when it comes to the situation of an alcoholic drinking again?

11. What is the curious mental phenomenon that precedes the first drink of the next series?

12. Is that behavior not absurd and incomprehensible if not plain insane? Explain.

13. Do you really agree with this statement, as it applies to you, that the alcoholic will absolutely be unable to stop drinking on the basis of self-know ledge alone?

14. Why do you believe or disbelieve that this is true in your own case?

15. What were the spiritual discoveries about alcoholism?

16. Explain this statement: *"The alcoholic, at certain times, has no mental defense against the first drink. Except in a few rare cases, neither he nor any other human being can provide such a defense. His defense must come from a Higher Power."*

Chapter Four - We Agnostics

1. Do you agree with the statement "…you may be suffering from an illness which only a *"spiritual experience"* can conquer" and if you do, explain what is true for you?

2. If an atheist's or agnostic's code of ethics or morals don't work, what decision must he or she make to achieve sobriety?

3. What is the main objective of the book *Alcoholics Anonymous?*

4. Why is a personal conception of a Higher Power so important for the atheist or agnostic?

5. What does this statement mean: *"Do not let any prejudice you may have against spiritual terms deter you from honestly asking yourself what they mean to you personally."*

6. Faced with alcoholic destruction, what did we do about spiritual matters?

7. What are some of the reasons the book gives for a belief in a Higher Power?

8. What have we learned about the frailties of various religious faiths?

9. What are the authors of the personal stories in the Big Book in total agreement about?

10. What was the proposition that we alcoholics had to face about God?

11. What was the *"great reality"* that we found deep down within ourselves?

12. What is the fundamental truth that is disclosed to us when we draw near to God?

Chapter Five - How It Works

1. What is the make-up of a person's constitution which causes them to fail to follow the AA Program??

2. What are those who fail naturally incapable of?

3. Why do the authors of the Big Book beg us to be fearless and thorough from the very start?

4. Why is it necessary to ask God's protection as we begin working the Twelve Steps?

5. Why are the Steps called a **suggested program** of recovery?

6. How do you practice each Step?

    Step 1 – We admitted we were powerless over alcohol – that our lives had become unmanageable.

    Step 2 – Came to believe that a Power Greater than ourselves could restore us to sanity.

    Step 3 – Made a decision to turn our will and our lives over to the care of God, as we understood Him.

    Step 4 – Made a searching and fearless moral inventory of ourselves.

Step 5 – Admitted to God, to ourselves, and to another human being the exact nature of our wrongs.

Step 6 – Were entirely ready to have God remove all these defects of character.

Step 7 – Humbly asked Him to remove our shortcomings.

Step 8 – Made a list of all the people we had harmed and became willing to make amends to them all.

Step 9 – Made direct amends to such people wherever possible, except when to do so would injure them or others.

Step 10 – Continued to take personal inventory and when we were wrong, promptly admitted it.

Step 11 – Sought through prayer and meditation to improve our conscious contact with God as we understood Him, asking only for knowledge of His will for us and the power to carry that out.

Step 12 – Having had a spiritual awakening as the result of these steps, we tried to carry this message to alcoholics and practice these principles in all our affairs.

7. What do we claim as the result of these steps?

8. What are the three pertinent ideas that were made clear as a result describing the alcoholic, the content of the Chapter to the Agnostics, and their personal adventures before and after?

A.

B.

C.

9. What is meant by turning our will and our life over to the care of God and how do we do that?

10. What do we have to be concerned about if we live our life based on self-will?

11. What delusion is the alcoholic a victim of?

12. Are you self-centered or ego-centric and what does that mean?

13. What do we need God's help for?

14. What are the two concepts that we had to accept?

   A.

   B.

15. When we took such a position, what kind of things started to happen?

16. The *"Third Step Prayer"* says: **"God, I offer myself to Thee to do with me as Thou will. Relieve me of the bondage of self, that I may better do Thy Will. Take away my difficulties, that victory over them will bear witness to those I would help of Thy Power, Thy Love, Thy way of life. May I do thy Will always."**
What does that prayer mean to you in your own life today?

17. They found it desirable to take this Step with whom?

18. What was the vigorous course of action to be taken following the taking of Step Three?

19. We realized that liquor was but a symptom of what was really wrong with us. What does getting down to causes and conditions mean to you?

20. What does a commercial inventory consist of/

21. What is the object of a *"personal"* moral inventory?

22. What personal flaws do we seek out/

23. What is meant by the statement: *"We have not only been mentally and physically ill, we have been spiritually sick"*?

24. What did they discover when they overcame their spiritual malady?

25. What is the main offender?

26. Have you taken a personal inventory the way it is described and illustrated in the Big Book? Why or why not?

27. Did you look at every item on the list and write down where you were to blame? Why or why not?

28. Have you reviewed your fears thoroughly and looked at every one of them to find out what is behind them?

29. What do we read over and over again in the Big Book about faith in God?

30. Have you learned about the real Power of God in your life? Explain.

Chapter Six - Into Action

1. What are you going to do about your personal inventory now that you have written it out?

2. What is the most difficult part of making the Fifth Step?

3. What are the consequences of skipping the Fifth Step?

4. What has the person who has skipped the Fifth Step not learned about its importance?

5. What kind of lives are alcoholics famous for living and why is that true?

6. We must be entirely honest with someone if we are to _____.

7. Who have you chosen to do this step with and why?

8. Why is a written inventory suggested as being necessary for taking the Fifth Step?

9. What is the effect, almost immediate, of taking this Step?

10. What do we do upon returning home after taking this Step?

11. What is the purpose of Step Six?

12. Why is it taken in the form of a prayer?

13. What is the Seventh Step Prayer?

14. What is meant by *"Faith without good works is dead"*?

15. What did we agree to be at the beginning?

16. How do we go out to our fellows and repair the damage we have done?

17. What if we don't have the will or the courage to face all the people in person that we have harmed?

18. What is the real purpose of making amends?

19. When we make amends, we are there to do what?

20. How do we manage money owed, criminal offenses committed, divorce and unpaid child support and alimony, and many other things we have done or failed to do?

21. We must not shrink from taking drastic action when called for and how do we handle each situations.....especially the more drastic ones?

22. Why does the Big Book say *"Our design for living is not a one way street"*?

23. Why is it that just staying sober ourselves is not sufficient amends?

24. What do we ask our creator each day in our meditation and prayer regarding or family life?

25. What are the Ninth Step Promises?

    A.

    B.

    C.

    D.

    E.

    F.

    G.

    H.

    I.

26. What is the suggestion of the Tenth Step?

27. What is our next objective now that we have thoroughly cleaned house and made amends?

28. Why does Step Ten have to be made every day for the rest of our lives?

29. What is our attitude about liquor?

30. What is the requirement for maintaining this new attitude/

31. What do we really have in regard to drinking?

32. Why do we say every day, *"How can I best serve Thee – Thy will, not mine be done"?*

33. Why is this daily commitment the proper use of our will?

34. Have you really become God-conscious?

35. We rely on daily prayer and meditation to guide our daily lives. What is
   A. Prayer

   B. Meditation

36. What do we do upon retiring at night?

37. What do we do upon awakening in the morning?

38. What do we do throughout the day?

39. What do we pray for?

40. Do we do our daily religious practices if our religion has them?

41. If we are agitated or doubtful during the day, what do we do?

42. Why do we say many times during the day, *"Thy Will be done"*?

43. Why does the book say at this point, *"But this is not all"*?

Chapter Seven - Working With Others

1. What has experience shown insures immunity from drinking?

2. What is the personal value obtained by working with others?

3. Why is working with others described as *"an experience you should not miss"*?

4. What is a good way to handle an alcoholic at first contact?

5. Why does it help if you tell some of your own story to a new man or woman?

6. Why should you stress that alcoholism is an "illness," a fatal malady?

7. What is the most important belief a person can have to help them conquer their alcohol problem?

8. Why should you help him or her that their religious convictions did not work to overcome their alcoholism?

9. Why didn't his or her religious convictions not work to overcome alcoholism?

10. Why do you just offer the friendship and fellowship of AA and not try to "sell" it to him or her?

11. Why do we find it a waste of time to chase a man or woman who will not do the work?

12. What may working with others mean to you?

13. Why is it important to help the families of alcoholics?

14. What is the most important thing to "burn" into the mind of the alcoholic?

15. Why is the family not essential to recovery?

16. What is the one thing to consider when going to a place where there is drinking?

17. Now that you are sober, what is your main job?

18. Why do you agree or disagree with the statement, "Our problems were of our own making. Bottles were only a symbol. Besides, we have stopped fighting anybody or anything. We have to?" What does that statement mean to you now?

Chapter Eight – To Wives

1. Why did the authors of the book emphasize that it was primarily written about men, but applied equally to women?

2. Why do you think a whole chapter written for the spouses, friends, and relatives of alcoholics?

3. What are some of the frustrations and problems mentioned by the wives of alcoholics"?

4. Why is it suggested that the alcoholic be treated as a "sick" person?

5. What are the four stages of alcoholism?

    Stage 1 –

    Stage 2 -

    Stage 3 -

    Stage 4 -

6. What is the First Principle of Success for handling an alcoholic spouse?

7. What is the Second Principle of Success for handling an alcoholic spouse?

8. What is the Third Principle of Success for handling an alcoholic spouse?

9. What is the Fourth Principle of Success for handling an alcoholic spouse?

10. Explain the incorporation of the spiritual program of AA into the Al-Anon Program.

11. What are some of the thoughts and emotions experienced by the spouse of alcoholics as they recover?

Chapter Nine - The Family Afterwards

1. Why is it suggested that all members of the family meet upon a common ground of tolerance, understanding, and love?

2. Do you agree that the cessation of drinking is but the first step away from the highly strained, abnormal condition of active alcoholism and that the whole family has been made ill?

3. What are some of the obstacles the family will meet over time?

4. Do you agree or disagree that all the members of the family, not just the alcoholic, are responsible for the recovery of the family? Why?

5. Why is the best place for the family to start with family recovery the spiritual aspect of the Program?

6. Why does the book say we are not a "glum lot" and insist that we enjoy life?

7. Why do we think that cheerfulness and laughter make for usefulness in family recovery?

8. Do you think that God wants us to be happy, joyous, and free? Why?

9. What is the most powerful health restorative for the alcoholic?

10. Why do we *not* disregard health matters?

11. What is the warning about sex relations?

12. What is suggested about re-establishing relations with our children?

13. What re the three "mottos" regarding the re-establishment of family life?
    A.

    B.

    C.

Chapter Ten - To Employers

1. Why is this chapter included in this book?

2. What does almost every modern employer feel about his employees?

3. Why is it so important to teach all employees that alcoholism is a disease?

4. How should the employer approach the person with a drinking problem?

5. Why is it so important that the employer read the Big Book?

Chapter Eleven - A Vision for You

1. What is it like to be subject to "King Alcohol"?

2. What are the "Four Horsemen" of alcoholism?

3. When will the "problem drinker" know loneliness as few people do?

4. Why does the "problem drinker' think he or she will be stupid, boring, and glum without alcohol?

5. How did you get to the fellowship of Alcoholics Anonymous?

6. Why do you think you have found the true meaning *of "Love your neighbor as you love yourself"*?

7. What does the book say is the most important thing to rely on for continuing sobriety?

8. Are you convinced that in order to live a sober life you must:
   A. Abandon yourself to God as you understand Him.

   B. Admit your faults to him and to your fellows.

   C. Clear away the wreckage of the past.

   D. Give freely of what you find.

   E. Join us as we trudge the road of happy destiny

   Explain.

NOTES

NOTES

NOTES

NOTES

Personal Stories

4th Edition

Part I – Pioneers of AA

Dr. Bob's Nightmare

What in this story relates to you?

What was the most important lesson or lessons did you learn from reading this story?

(1) Alcoholic Anonymous Number Three

What in this story relates to you?

What was the most important lesson or lessons did you learn from reading this story?

(2) Gratitude in Action

What in this story relates to you?

What was the most important lesson or lessons did you learn from reading this story?

(3) Women Suffer Too

What in this story relates to you?

What was the most important lesson or lessons did you learn from reading this story?

(4) Our Southern Friend

What in this story relates to you?

What was the most important lesson or lessons did you learn from reading this story?

(5) The Vicious Cycle

What in this story relates to you?

What was the most important lesson or lessons did you learn from reading this story?

(6) Jim's Story

What in this story relates to you?

What was the most important lesson or lessons did you learn from reading this story?

(7) The Man Who Mastered Fear

What in this story relates to you?

What was the most important lesson or lessons did you learn from reading this story?

(8) He Sold Himself Short

What in this story relates to you?

What was the most important lesson or lessons did you learn from reading this story?

(9) The Keys of the Kingdom

What in this story relates to you?

What was the most important lesson or lessons did you learn from reading this story?

Part II – They Stopped in Time

(1) The Missing Link

What in this story relates to you?

What was the most important lesson or lessons did you learn from reading this story?

(2) Fear of Fear

What in this story relates to you?

What was the most important lesson or lessons did you learn from reading this story?

(3) The Housewife Who Drank At Home

What in this story relates to you?

What was the most important lesson or lessons did you learn from reading this story?

(4) Physician Heal Thyself

What in this story relates to you?

What was the most important lesson or lessons did you learn from reading this story?

(5) My Chance to Live

What in this story relates to you?

What was the most important lesson or lessons did you learn from reading this story?

(6) Student of Life

What in this story relates to you?

What was the most important lesson or lessons did you learn from reading this story?

(7) Crossing the River of Denial

What in this story relates to you?

What was the most important lesson or lessons did you learn from reading this story?

(8) Because I'm an Alcoholic

What in this story relates to you?

What was the most important lesson or lessons did you learn from reading this story?

(9) It Might Have Been Worse

What in this story relates to you?

What was the most important lesson or lessons did you learn from reading this story?

(10) Tightrope

What in this story relates to you?

What was the most important lesson or lessons did you learn from reading this story?

(11) Flooded With Feeling

What in this story relates to you?

What was the most important lesson or lessons did you learn from reading this story?

(12) Winner Take All

What in this story relates to you?

What was the most important lesson or lessons did you learn from reading this story?

(13) Me an Alcoholic

What in this story relates to you?

What was the most important lesson or lessons did you learn from reading this story?

(14) The Perpetual Quest

What in this story relates to you?

What was the most important lesson or lessons did you learn from reading this story?

(15) A Drunk, Like You

What in this story relates to you?

What was the most important lesson or lessons did you learn from reading this story?

(16) Acceptance Was the Answer

What in this story relates to you?

What was the most important lesson or lessons did you learn from reading this story?

(17) Window of Opportunity

What in this story relates to you?

What was the most important lesson or lessons did you learn from reading this story?

Part III – They Lost Nearly All

(1) My Bottle, My Resentments, and Me

What in this story relates to you?

What was the most important lesson or lessons did you learn from reading this story?

(2) He Lived Only to Drink

What in this story relates to you?

What was the most important lesson or lessons did you learn from reading this story?

(3) Safe Haven

What in this story relates to you?

What was the most important lesson or lessons did you learn from reading this story?

(4) Listening to the Wind

What in this story relates to you?

What was the most important lesson or lessons did you learn from reading this story?

(5) Twice Gifted

What in this story relates to you?

What was the most important lesson or lessons did you learn from reading this story?

(6) Building a New Life

What in this story relates to you?

What was the most important lesson or lessons did you learn from reading this story?

(7) On the Move

What in this story relates to you?

What was the most important lesson or lessons did you learn from reading this story?

(8) A Vision of Recovery

What in this story relates to you?

What was the most important lesson or lessons did you learn from reading this story?

(9) Gutter Bravo

What in this story relates to you?

What was the most important lesson or lessons did you learn from reading this story?

(10) Empty on the Inside

What in this story relates to you?

What was the most important lesson or lessons did you learn from reading this story?

(11) Grounded

What in this story relates to you?

What was the most important lesson or lessons did you learn from reading this story?

(12) Another Chance

What in this story relates to you?

What was the most important lesson or lessons did you learn from reading this story?

(13) A Late Start

What in this story relates to you?

What was the most important lesson or lessons did you learn from reading this story?

(14) Freedom from Bondage

What in this story relates to you?

What was the most important lesson or lessons did you learn from reading this story?

(15) A.A. Taught Him to Handle Sobriety

What in this story relates to you?

What was the most important lesson or lessons did you learn from reading this story?

Publications

Alcoholics Anonymous Workbooks

"Alcoholics Anonymous Big Book Workbook"

> Createspace.com/3670322

> Amazon.com   ISBN 978-1466221222

"12 Steps and 12 Traditions and 12 Concepts of World Service"

> Createspace.com/3669631

> Amazon.com   ISBN 978-1466217270

"Spiritual Recovery Anonymous Workbook"

> Createspace.com/3921577
> Amazon.com   ISBN 978-1478143994

"Alcoholics Anonymous Comes of Age Workbook"

> Createspace.com/4766483

> Amazon.com   ISBN – 13:   978-1499184099

"Pass It On Workbook"

> Createspace.com/4766466

> Amazon.com   ISBN -13:   978-1499184044

"Came to Believe Workbook"

> Createspace.com/4766475

> Amazon.com   ISBN -13:   978-1466221222

"Dr. Bob and the Good Oldtimers Workbook"

> Createspace.com/4766487

> Amazon.com   ISBN -13:   978-1499184129

"Living Sober Workbook"

Createspace.com/4766470

Amazon.com   ISBN -13:   978-1499184068

Al-Anon Workbooks

"A Discovering Choices Workbook"
Createspace.com/3901579
Amazon.com   ISBN 978-1477615348

"A Family Group Workbook"
Createspace.com/3834681
Amazon.com   ISBN 978-1475582525

"A Paths to Recovery Twelve Step Workbook"

(Paths to Recovery – Pages 1 – 128)

Createspace.com/3857585
Amazon.com   ISBN 978-1475235616

"A Paths to Recovery Twelve Traditions Workbook"

(Paths to Recovery – Pages 131 - 240)
Createspace.com/3857611
Amazon.com   ISBN 978-1475235746

"A Paths to Recovery Twelve Concepts of World Service Workbook"
(Paths to Recovery – Pages 245 – 341)
Createspace.com/3857632
Amazon.com   ISBN 978-1475235852

"A Twelve Steps and Twelve Traditions Workbook"

Createspace.com/4497114

Amazon.com   ISBN -13:   978-1493582426

Golden Book Series Workbooks

"A Golden Book of Action Workbook"

Createspace.com/4494192

Amazon.com   ISBN -13:   978-1493581689

"A Golden Book of Attitudes Workbook"

Createspace.com/4494175

Amazon.com   ISBN -13:   978-1493581740

"A Golden Book of Decisions Workbook"

Createspace.com/4496990

Amazon.com   ISBN -13:   978-1493581634

"A Golden Book of Excuses Workbook"

Createspace.com/4497009

Amazon.com   ISBN -13:   978-1493581788

"A Golden Book of Happiness Workbook"

Createspace.com/4497020

Amazon.com   ISBN -13:   978-1493581818

"A Golden Book of Living Workbook"

Createspace.com/4497026

Amazon.com   ISBN -13:   978-1493581832

"A Golden Book of Passion Workbook"

Createspace.com/4497033

Amazon.com   ISBN -13:   978-1493581832

"A Golden Book of Principles Workbook"

Createspace.com/4497051

Amazon.com   ISBN -13:   978-1493581831

"A Golden Book of Resentments Workbook"

Createspace.com/4497051

Amazon.com   ISBN -13:   978-1493582037

"A Golden Book of Sanctity Workbook"

   Createspace.com/4807040

   Amazon.com   ISBN -13:   978-1499556100

"A Golden Book of Sanity Workbook"

   Createspace.com/4497068

   Amazon.com   ISBN -13:   978-1493582105

"A Golden Book of Sponsorship Workbook"

   Createspace.com/4497073

   Amazon.com   ISBN -13:   978-1493582143

"A Golden Book of the Spiritual Side Workbook"

   Createspace.com/4497077

   Amazon.com   ISBN -13:   978-1403582174

"A Golden Book of Tolerance Workbook"

   Createspace.com/4497085

   Amazon.com   ISBN -13:   978-1493582204

Books

"Adult Catholicism"

  Createspace.com/5176389

  Amazon.com   *ISBN 978-1505575859*

"Alcoholics Anonymous Sponsorship and Catholic Spiritual Direction"

  Createspace.com/4128360

  Amazon.com   ISBN – 13: 978-1481957892

"Alcoholism: A Fatally Progressive, Incurable Illness"

  Createspace.com/3938809

  Amazon.com   ISBN – 13: 978-1478252733

"Beyond the Twelve Steps"

  Createspace.com/3904184

  Amazon.com   ISBN – 13: 978-1477631751

"Beyond Human Power"

  Createspace.com/4507021

  Amazon.com   ISBN – 13: 978-1493646876

"Escape From Lapu-Lapu"

  Createspace.com/4149111

  Amazon.com   ISBN – 13: 978-148290277

"Fear of Death"

  Createspace.com/5282337

  Amazon.com   ISBN – 13: 978-1607733790

"Fear of God"

  Createspace.com/5106446

  Amazon.com   ISBN – 13: 978-1503233584

"God's Gatekeepers"

  Createspace.com/3923423

  Amazon.com   ISBN – 13: 978-1478156291

"Is Abortion Murder?"

  Createspace.com/4148680

  Amazon.com   ISBN – 13: 978-1482087475

"My AA Story"

Createspace.com/3708261

Amazon.com   ISBN – 13: 978-1466444607

"My AA Story: Part Two"

Createspace.com/3891033

Amazon.com   ISBN – 13: 978-1477547175

"My AA Story Continues On"

Createspace.com/3930623

Amazon.com   ISBN – 13: 978-1478201694

"My AA Story Trilogy"

Createspace.com/3942606

Amazon.com   ISBN – 13: 978-1478276333

"No Human Power"

Createspace.com/5043724

Amazon.com ISBN – 13: 978-1502785961

"On Being God's Miracle"

Createspace.com/3937092

Amazon.com   ISBN – 13: 978-1478241799

"Spiritual Awakening"

Createspace.com/4411734

Amazon.com ISBN – 13: 978-1493679034

"Spiritual Fitness"

Createspace.com/1502495334

Amazon.com   ISBN – 13: 978-1502495334

"Spirituality"

Createspace.com/5120357

Amazon.com   ISBN – 13: 978-1503337114

"Spiritual and Religion Addictions and Recovery"

Createspace.com/3916564

Amazon.com   ISBN – 13: 978-1478110258

"Spirituality and Religion in Alcoholics Anonymous"

Createspace.com/3907049

Amazon.com   ISBN – 13: 978-1477649985

"Spiritual Illness and Recovery"

Createspace.com/4037507

Amazon.com   ISBN – 13: 978-1480175258

"Spiritual Recovery: A Pathway to God"

Createspace.com/3867258

Amazon.com   ISBN – 13: 978-1475295375

"Spirituality and Religion in the Modern Age"

Createspace.com/4124691

Amazon.com   ISBN – 13: 978-1481935807

"The Spirituality of Sponsorship"

Createspace.com/3908571

Amazon.com   ISBN – 13: 978-1477659762

"The Twelve Steps of Spiritual Recovery"

Createspace.com/3889224

Amazon.com   ISBN – 13:   978-1477535400

"The Fourteen Rules of Spiritual Progress"

Createspace.com/3920252

Amazon.com   ISBN – 13: 978-1478135272

"The Miracle of Recovery"

Createspace.com/4516003

Amazon.com   ISBN – 13: 978-1493703371

"The Tenth Step"

Createspace.com/4131320

Amazon.com   ISBN – 13: 978-1481976329

"The Twelve Steps of Spiritual Progress"

Createspace.com/3889224

Amazon.com   ISBN – 13: 978-1477535400

Working the Steps"

Createspace.com/4135637

Amazon.com   ISBN – 13: 978-1482003062

"Spiritual Recovery Anonymous"
Createspace.com/3918035
Amazon.com   ISBN – 13: 978-1478120445